Creature

by Heidi Schreck

A SAMUEL FRENCH ACTING EDITION

SAMUEL FRENCH

FOUNDED 1830

NEW YORK HOLLYWOOD LONDON TORONTO

SAMUELFRENCH.COM

ISBN 978-0-573-69889-7   Printed in U.S.A.   #29667

MUSIC USE NOTE

Licensees are solely responsible for obtaining formal written permission from copyright owners to use copyrighted music in the performance of this play and are strongly cautioned to do so. If no such permission is obtained by the licensee, then the licensee must use only original music that the licensee owns and controls. Licensees are solely responsible and liable for all music clearances and shall indemnify the copyright owners of the play and their licensing agent, Samuel French, Inc., against any costs, expenses, losses and liabilities arising from the use of music by licensees.

IMPORTANT BILLING AND CREDIT REQUIREMENTS

All producers of *CREATURE must* give credit to the Author of the Play in all programs distributed in connection with performances of the Play, and in all instances in which the title of the Play appears for the purposes of advertising, publicizing or otherwise exploiting the Play and/or a production. The name of the Author *must* appear on a separate line on which no other name appears, immediately following the title and *must* appear in size of type not less than fifty percent of the size of the title type.

In addition the following credit *must* be given in all programs and publicity information distributed in association with this piece:

**The World Premiere of CREATURE was produced by
New Georges and Page 73 Productions**

CREATURE was first produced by Page 73 and New Georges Productions in New York City on October 27, 2009. The performance was directed by Leigh Silverman, with sets by Rachel Hauck, costumes by Theresa Squire, lighting by Matt Frey, and sound by Katie Down. The cast was as follows:

MARGERY KEMPE.	Sofia Jean Gomez
JOHN KEMPE	Darren Goldstein
FATHER THOMAS.	Jeremy Shamos
NURSE.	Tricia Rodley
ASMODEUS, JACOB	Will Rogers
JULIANA	Marylouise Burke

CHARACTERS

MARGERY KEMPE – the mayor's daughter
JOHN KEMPE – her husband
FATHER THOMAS – a priest
JULIANA – an anchoress
NURSE
JACOB – a young man
ASMODEUS – a devil (may be played by Jacob)
A HAZELNUT (to be played by Juliana)

SETTING

House of Margery Kempe and John Kempe
St. Margaret's Church
A choir loft
House of Father Thomas
Cell of Anchoress Juliana of Norwich
The outskirts of Lynn

TIME

Lynn, England: 1400-1401

AUTHOR'S NOTES

Although the play is set in 1400s England, it should be performed in contemporary American dialect. In that spirit, you might envision the world as a kind of collision between the contemporary and medieval imaginations, with all the freedom that implies. Please remain faithful to historical detail only to the extent that it inspires you.

PUNCTUATION NOTE

Two slash marks – // – indicate overlapping text. When the slash marks occur at the very end of a line, they signal a concise interruption.

*"He who has seen her comings and goings
knows that Love is the highest name of Hell."*
                                        Hadewijch of Brabant

Prologue:
"Her Table is Hunger"

(Lynn, England. 1400. A sick room in **MARGERY** *and* **JOHN KEMPE**'s *house.* **MARGERY**, *a beautiful young woman, is attended by her* **NURSE** *and* **ASMODEUS**, *a priest dressed in black.)*

NURSE. The doctor says you may not eat any beef, pork, goat's flesh, hare (which breeds incubi), conies, milk or anything that comes from milk, peacocks, pigeons, ducks, geese, swans, herons, cranes, coots, didappers, or fish of any kind. Eels are to be abhorred in all places at all times. Cabbage sends up black vapors to the brain and all salads breed melancholy – except bugloss and lettuce. Onions, garlic, scallions, turnips, carrots, radishes and parsnips are windy and bad and trouble the mind. All fruits such as pears, apples, plums, cherries, strawberries and nuts infect the blood and putrefy it. Also forbidden is pepper, cinnamon, cloves, honey and sugar, oil, vinegar, and salt.

MARGERY. When I do this, do I look like a snake? Ssssssith.

NURSE. Yes, miss.

MARGERY. Sssssith.

NURSE. Miss –

MARGERY. Sith! Sith!

(NURSE exits.)

MARGERY. Nurse.

NURSE. Yes, miss?

MARGERY. I want to see my baby.

(NURSE exits.)

ASMODEUS. How is your baby?

MARGERY. Oh. Forgive me, Father. I didn't see you there. Have you come to hear my confession?

ASMODEUS. Are you dying?

MARGERY. What?

ASMODEUS. You do your private penance, don't you?

MARGERY. ...There is a sin I have been carrying in my heart since I was a child —

ASMODEUS. Wait and confess it right before you die!

(beat)

MARGERY. Really? I thought –

ASMODEUS. Just an hour or so before you die, call for me. That way you won't have the shame of some priest knowing your secret while you're alive.

MARGERY. All right.

ASMODEUS. On the other hand, if you die suddenly – for example if you fall from a ladder –

MARGERY. If I fall from a –

ASMODEUS. Then what will happen to your soul?

(beat)

MARGERY. Forgive me father for I have sinned...

ASMODEUS. Wait, is it really horrible?

MARGERY. Um.

ASMODEUS. Sometimes, if the sin is really horrible, Hell will open up its mouth and swallow you immediately.

MARGERY. ...I think I'd like to wait.

ASMODEUS. Of course, if you wait, you might want to be careful around your baby. You know, because things can happen with babies.

MARGERY. What things?

ASMODEUS. Babies are conspicuously fragile. Sometimes if a little baby shows up who hasn't been baptized...Do you know if he *has* been baptized, by the way?

MARGERY. I've haven't seen my baby. I'm sick.

ASMODEUS. Yes, the puerperal fever, where the womb gets too moist and the brain fills up with water.

*(**ASMODEUS** makes slurping noises.)*

MARGERY. Ach! Stop it. Stop doing // that

ASMODEUS. It's always a good day when an unbaptized baby shows up because, well, babies are so cute, aren't they? Aren't babies cute?

MARGERY. ...Yes.

ASMODEUS. They're cute. And you can make them smile or you can make them cry. For example, if you poke one with a pin it will cry –

MARGERY. If you poke it with a pin –

ASMODEUS. Yes, if you poke it in the belly, the arm, the fingernail, or the eye it always lets out a little squeak – *eek* – or sometimes a shrill cry. *(He makes a horrific sound.)* Sometimes my brothers and I, we all gather around, pick up one baby and blow air into the baby like a balloon and then we play catch with it.

MARGERY. Where is my baby?

ASMODEUS. I don't know I haven't seen the little monster.

MARGERY. I want a real priest.

ASMODEUS. *(imitating her voice quite well)* "A real priest."

MARGERY. John.

ASMODEUS. Oh, John's out carousing again. You know. *With the boys.*

MARGERY. NURSE!

ASMODEUS. *(seductively)* I don't think Nurse likes you anymore. Do you want to look inside my mouth?

MARGERY. *(paralyzed)*...Why?

ASMODEUS. I'm going to open my mouth very wide and then you look in there. I think you'll be quite surprised by what you see.

(Sudden darkness. An unbearable shrieking. Lights up on **JOHN KEMPE** *slumped over a beer at large wooden table.)*

JOHN. WHAT THE HELL IS THAT? SOME KIND OF ANIMAL?

*(***NURSE*** *races in holding her hand up to her face. There is blood running down her cheek.)*

NURSE. It's your wife, she says there's a devil in her room and he's trying to swallow her.

JOHN. Oh for Christ's sake, again? Go and find her another priest.

NURSE. No one will see her —

JOHN. Get Father Walter, he's known her since she was a child.

NURSE. She bit him and now he won't come back.

JOHN. What about Father Robert?

NURSE. He says she tries to – to –

JOHN. To what?

NURSE. Tempt him?

JOHN. What?! He's nearly eighty! Can you get Father Allen?

NURSE. It's after midnight.

JOHN. Jesus Christ, find someone. Find her another idiot priest. I don't care who the Hell it is. Find someone who doesn't know her.

NURSE. Everyone in Lynn knows her.

JOHN. TRY NORFOLK.

NURSE. I'M A WOMAN I CAN'T TRAVEL BY MYSELF.

(*beat*)

JOHN. Oh no. Don't. Don't cry. Don't cry.

NURSE. I'm bleeding.

JOHN. Did she scratch your face? I'm sorry. Here…here's my napkin.

NURSE. I don't know if I can work here anymore.

JOHN. No no no. I'll go. I'm sorry I shouted. Stay here with the baby and I'll go.

NURSE. I don't want to be alone with her.

JOHN. Christ! I'll stay then, and you run down the road to Saint James. Find one of those smelly do-gooders who help the poor.

NURSE. …the *Greyfriars*?!

JOHN. Yes. Yes. Whoever. Tell them I'll make a donation.

NURSE. Yes, sir.

JOHN. Come back, though, won't you? Please don't leave us in this darkness.

Scene One

(MARGERY's sick room. ASMODEUS has been replaced by FATHER THOMAS, a gentle, somewhat nervous Grey-friar.)

FATHER THOMAS. Your husband says you need to make confession?

MARGERY. I wanted an old man priest. You look like a giant baby.

FATHER THOMAS. ...I'm thirty-five.

MARGERY. *(delighted)* Truly? Did you know that ever since I was a girl of twelve I have fallen passionately in love with men of thirty-five?

FATHER THOMAS. I don't know much about womanly things.

MARGERY. The first was a poet. And a banker. A poet and a banker. Well, in his heart he really was a poet – (would you hand me those crackers) – but his parents insisted that he become a banker because banking had been in his family for generations – banking and poetry. Don't you think that's a funny combination?

FATHER THOMAS. *(handing her the crackers)* Um //

MARGERY. *(eating crackers voraciously)* Cracker?

FATHER THOMAS. No, thank you //

MARGERY. *(conspiratorial)* They keep these things in the cellar which is quite damp, you know. The food is all rotten – it's moist and dripping with ooze. Ever since I stopped keeping the house it's all turned to muck. Have you ever eaten a rotten egg?

FATHER THOMAS. No.

MARGERY. You should try it! You should try eating a rotten egg!

FATHER THOMAS. How long has it been since your last confession?

MARGERY. What's your name.

FATHER THOMAS. Father Thomas.

MARGERY. *(indignant)* I've never heard of you!

FATHER THOMAS. I'm new to Lynn.

MARGERY. My Father was mayor of Lynn four times.

FATHER THOMAS. Your husband said that // you

MARGERY. Do you like baked eggs?

FATHER THOMAS. I do. // Yes.

MARGERY. Me too! Baked eggs with cheese! // Yum!

FATHER THOMAS. I've come to hear your confession.

MARGERY. Ha! You're a baby! If I start telling you my confession your head will blast into flames and you'll have to run to the river to put out the fire. It happened to Father Walter – didn't you hear? Don't you priests get together and gossip about the sinners?

FATHER THOMAS. No.

MARGERY. Liar.

FATHER THOMAS. I don't lie. It's a sin to lie.

MARGERY. *(flirtatious)* You're teasing me.

FATHER THOMAS. I'm not. We don't. We don't talk. We don't gossip about the sinners.

MARGERY. Come closer, I want to ask you something.

(He reluctantly moves closer.)

MARGERY. Closer. *(He moves closer.)* Do you know whether or not it's a sin to pray on your back?

FATHER THOMAS. Why do you ask?

MARGERY. Because I pray flat on my back, that's how I pray, and I want to know if that's why I'm being punished if that's why God is angry with me, because I pray on my back?

FATHER THOMAS. Well, it's not customary // certainly

MARGERY. I knew it! // I knew it!

FATHER THOMAS. but God wills us to pray in whatever way is most comfortable.

MARGERY. That's why that's why I am being punished! *(laughing)*

FATHER THOMAS. Do you want me to call the nurse?

MARGERY. *(laughing)* and I can't stop laughing – She has a face like a lemon. Don't you think she has a face like a lemon?

FATHER THOMAS. I didn't notice //

MARGERY. Or not like a lemon, but like the face a person makes when they eat a lemon?

*(**MARGERY** laughs and laughs. It's genuine and joyful, though it goes on a little too long.)*

FATHER THOMAS. MRS. KEMPE.

*(**MARGERY** stops laughing.)*

MARGERY. What?

FATHER THOMAS. *(hesitantly)* I know Divine Love…and I want that you should know it, too.

(beat)

MARGERY. HA HA HA HA HA HA HA HA HA HA.

*(**FATHER THOMAS** walks to the door.)*

MARGERY. Oh please forgive me! When you said those words – Div-Div – Divine ha ha ha oh oh oh I'm sorry! I'm sorry! I had a peculiar feeling!

FATHER THOMAS. It's nearly morning. If you don't need to confess, I'd rather go home to my bed than listen // to you.

MARGERY. Are you here because someone has died?

FATHER THOMAS. What?

MARGERY. Don't hide it from me. The sins of mothers are passed to babies // And then in Hell all of the devils play football using the babies as balls –

FATHER THOMAS. No, no. Mrs. Kempe, your baby is alive. Your baby is well. Your baby is well

MARGERY. …

FATHER THOMAS. *(clearly at a loss)* Would you like to… hold…your baby?

MARGERY. …

FATHER THOMAS. *(calling out the door)* NURSE! *(to* **MARGERY***)* Give me your hand.

(The **NURSE** *enters.)*

NURSE. Did you need help, Father?

FATHER THOMAS. Mrs. Kempe would like to see her –

MARGERY. No, no, I wouldn't.

(beat)

FATHER THOMAS. *(to* **NURSE***)* Could you bring her some water, please?

*(***NURSE** *exits.)*

FATHER THOMAS. How did you get this scar on your wrist?

MARGERY. I tried to bite out my veins.

FATHER THOMAS. Why?

MARGERY. Because I had no sword with which to smite off my own head. *(beat)* Please don't tell me despair is a sin. I know it is a sin.

FATHER THOMAS. Close your eyes and I'll pray for you.

*(***NURSE** *enters.)*

NURSE. Here's water, Father.

FATHER THOMAS. Thank you.

NURSE. Are you sure you don't need help with her?

MARGERY. *(whispering)* Lemon face, lemon face.

FATHER THOMAS. No, thank you.

*(***NURSE** *exits.)*

FATHER THOMAS. Drink some of this.

(He holds the cup for her as she drinks.)

MARGERY. Why through all of this horror has God never spoken to me?

FATHER THOMAS. He does not speak to us all, but that does not mean he loves us less.

MARGERY. Has He spoken to you?

FATHER THOMAS. *(nervously)* …I have had one revelation. Well it was not exactly a revelation because afterwards I did not know anything I had not known before…

MARGERY. What was it?

FATHER THOMAS. In a vision I saw the whole creation, that is, what is on this side and what is beyond the sea… And my soul in wonder cried out: "This world is pregnant with God."

(MARGERY giggles. FATHER THOMAS sighs.)

MARGERY. I'm sorry.

FATHER THOMAS. Let's ask Him to help you. Let's ask Him with all the strength of our hearts. Close your eyes. I'm right here.

(MARGERY closes her eyes and opens them again quickly. She closes them again.)

(a prayer)
Save her,
for the waters threaten her life;
She is wearied with calling,
her throat is parched;
Her eyes have failed
with looking for you…

(MARGERY begins softly snoring.)

(surprised, to God) Thank you.

(FATHER THOMAS blesses her. He exits. Outside the door, the NURSE can be heard singing the following song as the lights fade into a deep, lush darkness.)

NURSE. *(singing)*
WESTERN WIND, WHEN WILL THOU BLOW?
THE SMALL RAIN DOWN CAN RAIN.
CHRIST, THAT MY LOVE WERE IN MY ARMS,
AND I IN MY BED AGAIN.

(A loud knocking. MARGERY wakes.)

MARGERY. Who is that? What are you?

Um.

Jesus?

Oh! You are wearing purple, my favorite color.

I am?

Oh. Yes. Yes. I am. Yes, yes, yes. I am. I am. I am your –
I AM A CREATURE!

Scene Two

(The Kempe's main room. **JOHN** *stares in wonder at* **MARGERY** *who stands in the doorway wearing a stunning purple dress with slashed sleeves.)*

MARGERY. And then I said, "Who is it?" and someone said, "It's me!" And he sat down next to me on the bed and – hello Nurse, I'm cured and I'm telling John about the vision I had of Jesus Christ!

JOHN. You are astonishing! Where did you come from?

MARGERY. The mouth of Hell. Did you miss me?

(JOHN wraps himself around her.)

JOHN. Oh, yes. Yes, yes, yes, yes. //

MARGERY. Why don't I make us all something to eat? Some roast heron, perhaps? Or little ducklings in a sweet sauce? // Or thick sliced beefsteak with mounds of potatoes!

JOHN. No, no, no, little frog. //

MARGERY. I'll make your favorite fritters, John! Oooooooooooh yes! *(to* NURSE*)* Could I have my keys to the pantry please?

(NURSE looks at JOHN.)

(MARGERY looks at JOHN.)

Tell nurse to give me my keys.

JOHN. Margery, what do you need the keys for? Let nurse make you some roast meat and you stay here with me so I can kiss your little fingers and your little //

MARGERY. I want to run my house.

JOHN. Oh, come on little frog. Come here and sit on my lap. I want to look at you. Nurse, bring her some food please. She's famished.

NURSE. Certainly, sir…

MARGERY. AND A GIANT MUG OF BEER PLEASE.

(NURSE exits. JOHN *kisses* MARGERY *and pets her hair. Throughout the following exchange they cannot stop touching each other.)*

JOHN. You said evil things about me when you were possessed.

MARGERY. *(delighted)* I did what did I say?

JOHN. You said I was ugly.

MARGERY. It's not my fault, I was being tortured by devils.

JOHN. Do you want to see the baby? He's a little man already.

MARGERY. Does he love the Nurse more than me?

JOHN. You're his mother. Do you want to hold him?

MARGERY. …

JOHN. …

MARGERY. *(bright)* How is the brewery? Did you lose all our money?

JOHN. Half. I lost half our money.

MARGERY. Oooooh! Truly?

JOHN. I have a terrible head for business – I can't do it without you –

MARGERY. We have God, we don't need money! Oh John, if you only you had been in bed with me this morning and seen his sweet // face

JOHN. I was not allowed on account of being ugly and a demon —

MARGERY. I will become a saint! I'll be like Saint Bridget – people will travel from all over the world to hear about my visions—

JOHN. Margery, don't go // telling –

MARGERY. Oh, John, why did I ever choose to sin, when life is so merry in Heaven! How merry it is! How merry it is! HOW MERRY IT IS IN HEAVEN!

JOHN. Be calm —

MARGERY. *(singing poorly,* and *dancing a little)* HOW MERRY IT IS! HOW MERRY IT IS IN HEAVEN!

*(**NURSE** is heard screaming offstage.)*

JOHN. WHAT THE HELL?

(The baby starts crying. NURSE *enters.)*

NURSE. A HEDGEHOG, SIR. THERE'S A HEDGEHOG IN THE PANTRY.

JOHN. Oh for Christ's sake. Go back in there and chase it out.

NURSE. I won't sir. I won't go back in there. What if it's not just a hedgehog?

JOHN. What the Hell is it if it's not // just a hedgehog?

NURSE. A WITCH'S SERVANT!

JOHN. Oh good God in Heaven. You women and your watery brains –

MARGERY. I'll chase it out.

*(*MARGERY *exits.)*

JOHN. *(to* NURSE*)* I won't have superstitious twaddle in my house, you understand?

NURSE. I'm so sorry sir. It's my brother – he was telling // me

JOHN. *(whispering)* Do you really think she seems well?

NURSE. I didn't know her before sir.

JOHN. But doesn't she look amazing?

*(*MARGERY *enters.)*

MARGERY. There. That was the tiniest hedgehog I've ever seen. *(to* NURSE*)* I'm going to put it in a pie and serve it to you for supper. I'd like my keys now.

(Standoff. NURSE *slides the keys from her pocket, hands them to* JOHN *and exits to the kitchen.)*

MARGERY. *(serious)* John. Give me my keys.

JOHN. Will you sit on me again?

MARGERY. Give them to me.

JOHN. Come here my little saint and kiss me.

(She sits on his lap again. They have a quick wrestling match as she tries to get her keys. He pins her hands behind her back and kisses her.)

JOHN. Promise me you won't go telling all your friends about this miracle.

MARGERY. Why //

JOHN. You tell them it was just puerperal fever –

MARGERY. Ach! Stop // talking about –

JOHN. And now you're better. You don't talk about visions. You don't talk about the music of Heaven.

MARGERY. God is the master of my heart.

JOHN. Fine. Wonderful. But don't talk about it. Do you hear me? People will ridicule you. Or worse. You have to promise.

(beat)

MARGERY. Yes, I promise. Now will you give me my keys?

*(**JOHN** gives **MARGERY** the key to the pantry.)*

MARGERY. Do you know what I'm going to do with these?

(She mimes stabbing him in the heart.)

MARGERY. *(seductive)* I'm teasing you! Don't look at me like that. I'm going to open the pantry with these and then I'll make us Fritters. Yum! I'll take yolks of eggs, add flour and ale and stir it together till it be thick. Then I'll take pared apples, cut them thin like wafers, lay them in the batter, fry them in butter and serve them forth!

(He puts his hands under her dress and kisses her.)

MARGERY. *(seriously)* John. We sin too much.

JOHN. I know.

MARGERY. *(a troubling thought)* And what if God…what if He wants me to give you up?

(beat)

JOHN. You tell Him, I'll give you up when He does.

(She kisses him.)

MARGERY. Yes, John, yes, yes, yes, I'll tell him yes.

(Voices singing a three part Petronian motet, a kind of sacred chant, are heard. A tenor voice rises to prominence. Light reveals tenor, a beautiful young man named **JACOB**. *This is St. Margaret's church.)*

Scene Three

(**MARGERY** *enters St. Margaret's Church and looks up toward the cross.*)

MARGERY. Here I am.

I will do whatever you ask.

(*She waits a moment for something to be asked.*)

MARGERY. Um. I know that you gave Saint Mary of Oignes the gift of tears.

If you like, I can weep for you, too.

(*She begins to weep.*)

MARGERY. Oh, oh I am weeping. I am weeping!

(*She begins to weep loudly from happiness. The crying takes her by surprise. She experiments with escalating the sound. She wails. She begins to fall the ground. The beautiful young* **TENOR** *descends from the altar and catches her.*)

MARGERY. I don't know what's happening to me. Who are you?

JACOB. My name's Jacob.

MARGERY. The angel?

JACOB. No, Jacob wrestled with the angel, he wasn't an angel.

MARGERY. Oh.

JACOB. I'm just a man named Jacob. I come here in the mornings to pray before I go to work.

MARGERY. Can you hold onto me?

JACOB. Um, sure.

MARGERY. I'm having a kind of fit.

JACOB. I'm holding on to you.

Scene Four

(As **JACOB** *continues to hold* **MARGERY***, light reveals* **FATHER THOMAS** *reading in his cell.)*

FATHER THOMAS. What is sweetest in Love is her tempestuousness,
To die of hunger for her is to feed and taste;
Her despair is assurance;
Her sorest wounding is all curing
To waste away for her sake is to be in repose;
Her tender care enlarges our wounds
Her table is Hunger.

(**MARGERY** *leaves* **JACOB** *'s arms and walks to* **FATHER THOMAS***.)*

MARGERY. Do you live alone, then?

FATHER THOMAS. …With my mother….

(beat)

MARGERY. *(hesitantly)* I wanted to visit you earlier – to thank you – but I've been so busy.

FATHER THOMAS. I know, I hear that you pray – *loudly* – at St. Margaret's Church from early morning well into the evenings –

MARGERY. I am God's servant now.

FATHER THOMAS. And that you tell every person you meet about your vision of Christ in purple robes.

MARGERY. I'm going to become a saint.

(**FATHER THOMAS** *laughs.)*

MARGERY. What? Do you I think I'm too sinful?

FATHER THOMAS. No, no, no, you're not more than ordinarily sinful.

MARGERY. Then will you help me?

FATHER THOMAS. Oh. Well. I don't think it's the best use of our energies to *try* to become saints. I don't think this is what God asks of us.

MARGERY. Why not?

FATHER THOMAS. Also, most of the saints started their vocations when they were young —

MARGERY. Oh I'm ancient?

FATHER THOMAS. No. They were, however, mostly…

MARGERY. What? What?

FATHER THOMAS. Unmarried.

MARGERY. Not Saint Bridget!

FATHER THOMAS. No – but she was chaste.

MARGERY. Chaste?

FATHER THOMAS. My meaning is that you have your duties as a wife and a mother –

MARGERY. *(wrathful)* What do you mean I am ordinarily sinful? What are my ordinary sins?

FATHER THOMAS. There's wrath right there. And vanity – you might consider dressing with a little more humility considering how many poor people we having living in Lynne.

MARGERY. I have nothing but love for the poor! I feed little oat cakes to the poor every day of the week at my house! No one in Lynn treats the poor better than I do.

FATHER THOMAS. Well, maybe not in Lynn, but you want to be a saint. Mary of Oignes gave away everything she had to the poor and then begged in order to feed them. Catherine of Siena drank the pus of lepers. Would you do that?

(beat)

MARGERY. Yes.

FATHER THOMAS. …

MARGERY. Will you please teach me how to be less sinful?

FATHER THOMAS. You think too highly of me. You should go to Father Walter.

MARGERY. Father Walter told me I was going to Hell.

FATHER THOMAS. He said you were going to —

MARGERY. Do you know much about Hell?

FATHER THOMAS. I know what the scriptures tell me. And I have meditated on it.

MARGERY. You have meditated on it! You have meditated on Hell?

FATHER THOMAS. Yes.

MARGERY. What did you see?

FATHER THOMAS. Um.

MARGERY. And what does it mean exactly, meditating? I mean, what is it you do?

FATHER THOMAS. …First you just find a comfortable position and breathe. You concentrate on your breath for a while – why did Father Walter tell you were going to Hell?

(beat)

MARGERY. God doesn't like Father Walter. He told me that I should visit you.

FATHER THOMAS. He did?

MARGERY. He says hello.

FATHER THOMAS. Hello?

MARGERY. Yes, He says hello and that you greatly please him and that I am to tell you all the secrets of my soul.

(beat)

FATHER THOMAS. Mrs. Kempe, I'm not a teacher. I've been called to help the poor – to give comfort to those who have nothing –

MARGERY. *I* am poor! *I* have nothing!

FATHER THOMAS. You have a husband and a baby and also from what I hear a highly profitable beer business.

MARGERY. I am poor in spirit!

FATHER THOMAS. You had a vision from the Lord God, the kind of visitation that some people have prayed their entire lives to perceive! Some people have prayed with utter humility to behold the vision that you – a woman with no learning, no conspicuous virtues. //

MARGERY. I know that I am not virtuous!

FATHER THOMAS. And yet you awoke one morning to a vision of Jesus Christ in purple – purple? Robes?

MARGERY. Yes, yes, yes, I am rich in His love and I am bringing it to you. Look at me. I am bringing it to you —

FATHER THOMAS. Please stand up!

MARGERY. Who is poorer than I? You said before I'm wrathful and vain. It's true. I have no humility, no generosity, no *temperance* and yet every day I must keep living! I must live on and on and on drinking beer and stuffing myself full of meat. Whereas you – you devote your life to helping the poor, and God, He is so proud of you. He told me that! He told me that you are kind and good, and that you will continue to live in this blessed goodness for seven more years, and then after seven years, you will die a respected and holy...man...

FATHER THOMAS. ...

MARGERY. I'm sorry. Perhaps I heard it wrong?

FATHER THOMAS. ...What else does He say to you?

MARGERY. He says...I should ask Him for no more than love – for only love can win what it wills.

FATHER THOMAS. What does that mean, "only love can win what it wills?"

MARGERY. I don't know. You're the priest.

FATHER THOMAS. ...I'll think on it.

MARGERY. Please help me. My friends think I'm a liar. And I'm not allowed to listen to the sermons at St. Margaret's anymore because of my weeping.

FATHER THOMAS. Why do you weep?

MARGERY. Because my heart is burning up. And I want to put out the fire by flinging myself upon on the beautiful things that God has made.

(*uncomfortable beat*)

FATHER THOMAS. ...There's an anchoress called Juliana who has had visions like yours.

MARGERY. Is she married?

FATHER THOMAS. No. No. She lives in a little room attached to the Church at Norwich. She hasn't left the room for thirty years. She just sits in there and thinks on God.

MARGERY. How does she eat?

FATHER THOMAS. People bring her food. Her followers.

MARGERY. I'd like to live in a little house and have my followers bring me food. Though it depends on what kind of food they bring. I love honey cakes.

FATHER THOMAS. I have a book of her revelations.

(He finds and hands her a book.)

MARGERY. Oh, pretty.

FATHER THOMAS. Open it. Why don't you take it with you and read it.

MARGERY. …

FATHER THOMAS. Or perhaps your husband could read it to // you

MARGERY. Read to me.

FATHER THOMAS. What? No, I //

MARGERY. Please.

FATHER THOMAS. We have too many sick people today –

MARGERY. I'll help you. I'll give you money. I'll make soup for the sick people. I'll – I'll press a cool cloth to their burning foreheads. I'll, um, suck the…ooze // from their –

FATHER THOMAS. All right. The soup will suffice – and maybe a donation. Here. *(looking at the page)* This is from her fourth vision, one of my favorites. "In our fleeting life here on earth –" Ahem. *(reading a little louder)* "In our fleeting life here on earth, our soul knoweth not what our Self is."

(beat)

Did He tell you how I would die?

MARGERY. He said you would die a good man.

FATHER THOMAS. "In our fleeting life here on earth –" *(beat)* I have an English Bible. We could read from that, too.

MARGERY. An English Bible?

FATHER THOMAS. Don't tell anyone. *(beat)* "In our fleeting life here on earth…"

(Light reveals **JULIANA** *in her cell, eating a honey cake.)*

JULIANA. In our fleeting life here on earth, our soul knoweth not what our Self is: When we clearly see what our Self is, then we shall truly know God. But we may never fully know our Self until the last point – the point at which this fleeting, painful life shall end.

Scene Five

(JOHN and MARGERY KEMPE's house. JOHN sits at the table writing a letter for an enraged MARGERY, who shouts to him from the pantry.)

JOHN. Margery, you'll have no friends left!

MARGERY. *(offstage)* Write it John! Write: "Remember, *Anne,* that you will never have the grace that this creature has. *Never.*"

JOHN. Will you make love to me if I write it?

MARGERY. *(offstage)* John, stop it! I must make her understand!

JOHN. Understand what?

(MARGERY enters wearing a long black shift. Her hair is covered by a scarf.)

MARGERY. That *I* am the one God is speaking to, not her. That *I* am the one God loves. Why does she insult me when *I* am the one God is speaking to //

JOHN. What are you wearing?

MARGERY. I am dressing with more humility!

JOHN. If there was a man with a sword who was going to smite off my head if I didn't make love to you – would you allow my head to be smit off?

MARGERY. John, we have succeeded in being chaste for eight weeks. Why are you bringing this up now?

(beat)

JOHN. What do I write again?

MARGERY. "Dear Anne. You will never have the grace that this creature has."

JOHN. "Dear Anne. You will never have the grace that I, Margery, have."

MARGERY. No! Start over.

JOHN. That's money!

MARGERY. It's fine, we can afford it.

JOHN. You're bankrupting us! We've got nothing left! That old man you hired is a bandit and a demon has gotten into the horses –

MARGERY. Who says that? // Who says a demon has gotten into the horses?

JOHN. Everyone! You make a new enemy every day—

MARGERY. *(dictating)* DEAR ANNE YOU WILL NEVER HAVE THE GRACE! //

(**JOHN** *sighs and goes back to writing. At some point during the following argument, the* **NURSE** *enters sees that they are fighting [again] and quickly exits.*)

JOHN. …you will never have the grace…

MARGERY. *(indicating herself)* *This* creature has.

(**JOHN** *writes.*)

MARGERY. "For God has told me that He would be right well pleased if I never set foot in your house again."

JOHN. *(as he's writing)* Oh for Christs's sake!

MARGERY. Christ died for your sins, John, and every time you curse He dies again.

JOHN. She's your last friend, Margery –

MARGERY. How dare she say I am a liar when I am only trying to help? It is my holy duty to save my friends from sin, it is my *duty* John.

JOHN. Yes, yes –

MARGERY. Is it my fault she has not paid enough indulgences and her husband is rotting in purgatory?

JOHN. Margery!

MARGERY. Please write: "Madame our Lord Jesus Christ wants me to tell you that your husband is ROTTING IN PURGATORY –"

JOHN. "Madame, our Lord Jesus Christ wants me –"

MARGERY. "…and that it will be A VERY LONG TIME before he ascends to Heaven."

(Pause. **JOHN** *finishes the letter.)*

JOHN. There. That's sufficient don't you think. Will you put your signature?

MARGERY. Yes.

(She moves to sign it. Hesitates.)

MARGERY. Will you show me how again?

JOHN. *(showing her)* M A-R-G-E-R-Y.

MARGERY. My hand's tired. Will you write Kempe?

JOHN. Yes. *(He does.)* How's that?

MARGERY. Thank you.

JOHN. Give me your hand. *(He massages it.)* God does not need to be spoken of every moment for His presence to be felt. You swore to me that you wouldn't speak of it, and now you talk of nothing else.

MARGERY. Stop touching me. I had rather see your head smit off than we should turn again to our uncleanness.

*(**JOHN** rips up the letter.)*

You'll regret that, John. When the devils are boiling you alive in an enormous pot.

*(**MARGERY** deliberately picks up a bowl of hazelnuts and hurls them across the room. She exits. **JOHN** gets up to follow her then changes his mind. **NURSE** enters sees the hazelnuts and exits. She returns with a broom and begins to sweep them up.)*

JOHN. Leave those for my wife to clean up.

NURSE. Yes, sir.

JOHN. Come here for a moment.

*(**NURSE** walks to him.)*

JOHN. Do you pity me?

NURSE. Why should I, sir?

JOHN. You don't then?

NURSE. …

JOHN. Why don't you sit on my lap?

*(**NURSE** hesitates a moment before sitting on his lap. He puts his arms around her.)*

JOHN. Is this good?

NURSE. …Yes.

JOHN. Are you a witch?

NURSE. What, sir?

JOHN. Are you perhaps bewitching my wife? I see you sewing little things all the time. What are those packets you're sewing? Do you put little bones in there? Do you hide little bits of animal and then cast spells to poison my wife's soul?

NURSE. Those are nightclothes I'm sewing. For your son.

(JOHN *presses his face into* NURSE*'s stomach.* NURSE *moves away quickly and stands.*)

NURSE. I should look after the baby.

JOHN. Then will you bring me something to eat?

NURSE. Certainly, sir.

JOHN. And more beer?

(NURSE *exits.*)

Scene Six

(Low chanting. In the choir loft of St. Margaret's church,
MARGERY *is wailing alone on her back, like a baby. She*
sees **JACOB** *and abruptly stops.)*

JACOB. Were you weeping?

MARGERY. *(perfectly all right)* Yes.

JACOB. I'm Jacob – Jacob, the man. I followed you here. I
wanted to hear you weep again. The first time I heard
you wailing I felt something – It felt like my heart was
burning.

MARGERY. That happens to me too.

JACOB. No, I mean later, when I put my hand on my chest,
it was actually hot to the touch. And then I took off my
shirt and there was a red mark in the shape of a heart
on my skin. Has that ever happened to you?

MARGERY. ...No.

JACOB. I know your weeping is a gift from Him. I've
learned that I must adore Him with all the strength of
my being.

MARGERY. That's true.

JACOB. Are you ever frightened?

MARGERY. By what?

JACOB. Some people think you're a Lollard. And they're
arresting Lollards now – I hear they're cleaning them
out of Oxford.

MARGERY. Cleaning?

JACOB. Yes, and they're burning William Sautre in Smithfield next week. I'm thinking of going. It's historic.

MARGERY. What's a – Who says I'm a Lollard?

JACOB. My friends. They say you're lying about your vision
– and sometimes you eat meat on Fridays.

(beat)

They're idiots.

MARGERY. I'm not a –

JACOB. I know. You're perfect.

    (Beat. She is tempted by this idea.)

MARGERY. Oh, thank you, but–. I don't know if I'm…

JACOB. Yes. You are. You are astonishing.

    (beat)

MARGERY. Could I tell you a secret?

JACOB. Yes.

MARGERY. When I was younger I was very wicked.

JACOB. I don't believe you.

MARGERY. After this life, it's important that I go some place where I can really just rest.

JACOB. Oh, you're crying!

MARGERY. It is impossible for me to look at the face of a boy without thinking of Christ's suffering.

JACOB. I'm a man. I'm twenty.

MARGERY. Of course. I'm sorry.

JACOB. You see Him when you look at me?

MARGERY. *(wiping her eyes)* Yes I do.

    (JACOB *grabs her hand and puts it on his cheek.)*

MARGERY. I should be going. I haven't eaten.

JACOB. *(taking a little bag from his belt)* Will you accept these figs from me?

MARGERY. Oh, no, I can't.

JACOB. Please.

MARGERY. I can't. I can't.

JACOB. Please, take these figs. They're imported. From Heaven. I'm just teasing. Remember, because of how you thought I was an angel…

MARGERY. *(taking the figs)* Thank you.

JACOB. Let me walk you home.

MARGERY. I'm visiting a priest. My teacher.

JACOB. I'll wait outside your teacher's house so I can walk you home and protect you from those idiots who say you're a Lollard –

MARGERY. I'm not afraid. I would endure anything for the sake of this Love.

JACOB. I would endure anything for the sake of your love.

   (beat)

MARGERY. You can walk with me, but you can't talk to me of love.

JACOB. No. No. I won't. I won't talk of love. I won't. I won't talk of love.

Scene Seven

*(NURSE's closet. She is frantically opening small bags
and dumping bones onto the floor.)*

NURSE. St. Bridget, please help me, I know not what I do.
It's true I meddled in witchcraft but I'm no witch. I
sewed a bag together with little bones in it and placed
it under the door jam. I did this because I love him.
I tried to love her, too, in order to make his life less
miserable, but I am incapable of such a love. I am
unworthy even to crawl upon this earth. But I am no
witch. My love was something pure which became
rotten. I wanted to love him with my body because,
well...I have nothing else with which to love.

One, two, three, four, five –.I'm missing one. I'm missing one bag. I'M MISSING ONE BAG.

I meddled in it because I didn't believe in it. Or maybe
I did believe. I saw one day that I might have power.
One day I was walking by the house of a woman who
had aggrieved me greatly and while walking by I was
thinking terrible thoughts about her when she happened to come out onto her porch I cast my eyes upon
her and straightaway she vomited.

Scene Eight

(**MARGERY** *sits in* **FATHER THOMAS**'s *cell eating from the bag of figs* **JACOB** *gave her. She seems a bit troubled.* **FATHER THOMAS** *reads to her from* **JULIANA**'s *book. He is good at reading to her now – and he proclaims with a great deal of enthusiasm.*)

FATHER THOMAS. "And after this, I saw God in a point, that is, in my understanding. I saw that he is in all things. And I marveled at that sight with a soft dread and thought, 'What is sin?'"

MARGERY. What's a *Lollard*?

FATHER THOMAS. What? Why are you asking?

MARGERY. They're cleaning them out of Oxford.

FATHER THOMAS. Cleaning?

MARGERY. Yes.

FATHER THOMAS. Who told you that?

MARGERY. Jacob.

FATHER THOMAS. Who's Jacob?

MARGERY. He says they're burning a man in Smithfield next week.

FATHER THOMAS. That's true. I'm going to see it.

MARGERY. Because it's historic?

FATHER THOMAS. No. Because I don't want to shut my eyes to the horrors that are being committed in God's name.

MARGERY. Jacob wants to go because it's historic.

FATHER THOMAS. Who's Jacob?

MARGERY. I met him at church. What's a Lollard.

FATHER THOMAS. A Lollard is a person who believes that he does not need the church to worship God.

MARGERY. Oh. I believe that.

FATHER THOMAS. It's not always prudent to say what you believe.

MARGERY. But maybe I'm a Lollard.

FATHER THOMAS. No you're not. A Lollard doesn't believe that bread becomes the body of Christ.

MARGERY. That's ridiculous, of course it does!

FATHER THOMAS. Well, then you're not a Lollard //

MARGERY. What else do crazy Lollards believe?

FATHER THOMAS. They believe – don't call them crazy Lollards. They believe that a person should be able to read the word of God without the help of a priest. It is because of them that I can read to you from an English Bible.

MARGERY. Did you get your Bible from a LOLLARD?

FATHER THOMAS. You didn't even know what a Lollard was before this moment, so please stop using that voice.

MARGERY. But aren't Lollards heretics?!

FATHER THOMAS. Who told you that? All this hysteria about Lollards – you're talking like an idiot.

MARGERY. *(hurt)* I'm not an idiot. Jacob says that I'm astonishing. My weeping gives him faith.

FATHER THOMAS. ...Your weeping gives me faith, too.

MARGERY. *(genuinely surprised)* It does?

FATHER THOMAS. Yes. I had my vision when I was ten, but I can't truly remember it. I *thought* I was filled with something – but I only remember that I cried out, "This world is pregnant with God." I remember the words, but absolutely nothing of the feeling remains. *This world is pregnant with God.*

MARGERY. *This world is pregnant with God.*

FATHER THOMAS. Does it give you any kind of feeling?

(beat)

MARGERY. No. Nothing.

FATHER THOMAS. When you weep, when you tell me the things God said to you, I feel near to Him. As near to Him as I may ever be.

(tender yet uncomfortable sort of beat)

MARGERY. I...I brought some figs for your mother.

FATHER THOMAS. Thank you. That was thoughtful.

(*MARGERY sets the figs down. She smiles at* **FATHER THOMAS** *– it's radiant, overwhelming.*)

MARGERY. May I see the book?

(**FATHER THOMAS** *hands her the book.*)

Juuuu-liiiiiii-aaaaaaaa-naaaaaaaa. Margery. Margery. Mrgry.

FATHER THOMAS. It's a fine name.

MARGERY. For a saint?

FATHER THOMAS. Margery…

MARGERY. I'd like to bring her a honey cake.

FATHER THOMAS. Perhaps one day you can make a pilgrimage.

MARGERY. Will you take me?

FATHER THOMAS. To Norwich? Oh, I don't think that would be —

MARGERY. I can't travel by myself.

FATHER THOMAS. …You should ask your husband to take you.

(**MARGERY** *looks at the book.*)

MARGERY. She's wearing all white.

FATHER THOMAS. Yes.

MARGERY. I want to wear white.

FATHER THOMAS. What? You're married. People will think –

MARGERY. God has spoken to me. He has not spoken to them.

FATHER THOMAS. Yes, but you're not…

MARGERY. What?

FATHER THOMAS. You're a mother.

MARGERY. I belong to God.

(*Silence as* **FATHER THOMAS** *perceives this truth.*)

MARGERY. And one day he will burn up all my enemies in a giant fire.

FATHER THOMAS. …

MARGERY. Do you think your mother would be angry if we ate a couple of her figs?

FATHER THOMAS. You've been eating them.

MARGERY. I have?

FATHER THOMAS. Yes.

MARGERY. Take them away from me. You eat them.

FATHER THOMAS. Thank you, but I'm fasting.

MARGERY. Oh. Will I become a saint more quickly if I fast?

FATHER THOMAS. Well, usually we fast to relieve the suffering of those who are in purgatory, not to help ourselves.

MARGERY. Oh.

FATHER THOMAS. But fasting can also help you…take your eyes off the things of this world.

MARGERY. Please, will you give me permission to wear white?

FATHER THOMAS. You should ask someone with a little more authority.

MARGERY. Who? Father Walter? He was afraid to hear my confession.

FATHER THOMAS. With all due respect to Father Walter, I would be happy to hear your confession.

MARGERY. …

FATHER THOMAS. One of the reasons we confess to other people is so that we can help one another – here on earth. We confess because sin is heavy and we are so… fragile.

(beat)

MARGERY. Would you like to confess to me, then?

FATHER THOMAS. Oh, well, I don't think –

MARGERY. You don't want the shame of me knowing your secrets?

(beat)

FATHER THOMAS. Well all right. Um…My brother. Once when he was small I told him that we all pass into nothingness. He was only five and I was older and should have known better. He cried and cried and I could see that he believed there was no Heaven, no God, that we would, Mother, Father, all of us one day become nothing. Later that day he was struck on the head. Some workmen let a stone fall from a house they were building, and he died immediately. He died a non-believer. He died a heretic.

MARGERY. …

FATHER THOMAS. Would you like to try now.

(long beat)

MARGERY. To whom do I belong first? To my husband or to God?

FATHER THOMAS. …to God.

MARGERY. Then may I please wear white?

FATHER THOMAS. That is between you and God.

MARGERY. Forgive me Father, for I have sinned. When I was ten years old and didn't know any better…Pah. Pah.

(MARGERY looks as if she is about to vomit.)

FATHER THOMAS. Are you well?

MARGERY. I have a sweet taste in my mouth – it's so – pah pah, it's so syrupy, yeck.

FATHER THOMAS. Margery?

MARGERY. *(a crazy relief)* ahhhhhhhhhhhhhhhhhh-hhhhhhhhhhhhhhhhhhhh, it's not syrupy, it's goooooooooooooooooooood, oh dear god, dear god dear god, thank you —

FATHER THOMAS. Are you —

MARGERY. THE FIGS!

FATHER THOMAS. What?

MARGERY. Yes, yes, yes! They ARE from Heaven! Oh Father. Father. Taste.

(MARGERY moves to kiss FATHER THOMAS, falls to the floor and begins to writhe and weep loudly.)

(**FATHER THOMAS** *kneels down to calm her and they become a medieval painting.* **JACOB** *is heard singing ecstatic music. Darkness. The song continues.* **MARGERY** *standing before the cross. She ferociously rips off her head covering and dress. Underneath she is wearing all white. She is on fire with the Holy Spirit and she looks like a demon. A clanging of bells.*)

Scene Nine

(**MARGERY** *at the kitchen table in her white dress, praying. The hazelnuts have been swept into a pile in the corner of the room.*)

MARGERY. *(fierce)* I'll ask nurse to bring me a steak. I'll ask nurse to bring me a piece of bread. I'll have one piece of bread and that's all. That's it. Maybe I'll just have one piece of bread now. One piece of bread is that breaking a fast? I don't think so. Nurse! No no nevermind. NEVERMIND NURSE. I'll wait until one minute after midnight and then I'll have a steak medium rare and a mug of beer and that's all.

NURSE, COULD YOU BRING ME SOME HERRING?! Oh, I'm having that needle feeling, I'm having that needle feeling Jacob talked about. Jacob. Jacob. NURSE, NEVERMIND. I'll wait until one minute after midnight and then I'll have a steak, a mug of beer and creamy potatoes. Mmmmmmmmmmmmm creamy potatoes. (**MARGERY** *licks the table.*) NURSE? Oh my heart. My heart is burning up, I wonder if there is the shape of a heart burnt onto my chest. I feel it I can feel it I can feel that there is (**MARGERY** *puts her hands inside her dress.*) It's hot! It's hot to the touch!

(**NURSE** *enters. She is terrified when she sees* **MARGERY** *with her hands inside her dress.*)

IT'S MY NEW DRESS, IT STILL HAS A PIN STUCK IN IT!

NURSE. Oh.

MARGERY. I was pulling out the pin. Oh, here's the pin. There was a pin in my dress. *(Miraculously, there is a pin.)* See?

NURSE. Yes.

MARGERY. *(terrified)* What did you think it was, a devil?

NURSE. *(also terrified)* Yes, I'm sorry I did. Forgive me. It's only because my brother says there are more devils than usual out this season. He's seen some women out on the edge of town –

MARGERY. *(even more terrified)* On the edge of town? Doing what?

NURSE. *(escalating)* Well they're – they have their legs up in the air as if they're you know – being *attacked* by demons.

MARGERY. WHAT?

NURSE. He's superstitious.

MARGERY. Oh.

NURSE. Here's your herring.

MARGERY. I don't – thank you. Your brother – did he actually see these demons?

NURSE. No, he says they're invisible. You can only see the women. They're moving around you know with their… with their legs up in the air and they're moaning… with pleasure, but you can't see the demon. That's what's so terrifying.

MARGERY. But can the woman see the demon?

NURSE. I don't know, miss. Can I bring you anything else?

MARGERY. Yes. No. No. Yes. No. No, thank you.

(NURSE exits.)

*(Still at the table **MARGERY** prays.)*

False flesh, you shall eat no herring. False flesh, you shall eat no herring. NURSE NURSE NURSE!

(NURSE enters.)

I want a steak.

NURSE. Yes, miss.

(NURSE exits.)

MARGERY. NURSE?

(NURSE enters.)

NURSE. Yes?

(beat)

MARGERY. Would you tell me your real name?

(beat)

NURSE. Eliza.

MARGERY. Eliza – "I have never experienced Love in any sort of way as repose. For me Love has always been terrible and implacable, devouring and burning..."

NURSE. ...

NURSE. "Since you are a human being, live in misery as a human being."

NURSE. It's something my mother used to say.

NURSE. ...

MARGERY. ...

NURSE. Can I bring you anything else besides the steak?

MARGERY. No, thank you. Jacob will be coming by soon to take me to church. Could you let me know when he arrives?

NURSE. That little poplet, miss?

MARGERY. He's nearly twenty.

NURSE. Hm.

(**NURSE** *exits.* **MARGERY** *begins to devour the herring. A voice comes from the pile of hazelnuts.*)

JULIANA. Look at me.

MARGERY. *(with a mouthful of herring)* What?

JULIANA. Over here. Look at this little thing over here that was created.

MARGERY. What are you?

JULIANA. A hazelnut. What are you?

MARGERY. A woman.

JULIANA. Aren't you amazed that I can last, for don't you think that because of my littleness that I would suddenly have fallen into nothing? But look at me! I last and I always will, because God loves me. Come over here and look at me.

(**MARGERY** *moves slowly toward the hazelnuts.*)

Look at me. You will see three properties. The first is that God made me; the second is that God loves me; the third is that God preserves me. But what else do you see?

(**MARGERY** *picks up a hazelnut and looks at it.*)

MARGERY. ...

JULIANA. I know you are only a woman, but try to think a little harder.

(sound of the baby crying)

MARGERY. I can't.

(The **HAZLENUT** *exits, disappointed. The sound of the crying baby is revealed to be* **ASMODEUS.***)*

MARGERY. What are you.

ASMODEUS. *(very cute)* I'm a baaaaaaaaby. Waaaaaaaaaa! Waaaaaaaaaaaaaaa!

MARGERY. Stop that.

ASMODEUS. I need some milk!

(He makes a slurping sound.)

MARGERY. Ach, stop it. Stop talking about —

(ASMODEUS *laughs joyfully. In a swift motion removes his hood, revealing two little devil horns.)*

ASMODEUS. I'M NOT A BABY!

(ASMODEUS *proudly models his devil costume.)*

Do you like my costume? In reality, I'm just a hulking mass of shadow. Dark gray without substance. This here is what I'm wearing for the Mystery Pageant. They finally let me play a devil.

(MARGERY *climbs on to the floor and begins to pray frantically on her back.)*

I like your costume, too.

(MARGERY *begins to pray more loudly.)*

What are you supposed to be anyway?

(MARGERY *prays even more loudly.)*

DON'T PRAY LIKE THAT. YOU'LL END UP IN HELL.

MARGERY. FATHER THOMAS TOLD ME I COULD PRAY ANY WAY I CHOOSE.

ASMODEUS. Father Thomas is not a particularly powerful priest is he?

MARGERY. ...No

ASMODEUS. Maybe you should ask somebody with a little more *authority*.

MARGERY. *(not totally understanding the word)* God loves me and He knows me.

ASMODEUS. Oh, have you had more visions?

MARGERY. ...No.

ASMODEUS. How do you know he loves you then?

MARGERY. He told me.

ASMODEUS. Just that one time?

MARGERY. ...Yes.

ASMODEUS. Let me consult an authority. I have a little book here.

MARGERY. What is it?

ASMODEUS. It's the Devil's Book. Let me open it up. Oh. Oh. Look here's your name. On this page is written a little story about you. Oh. Oh dear. *(reading)* Oh this is horrible. This is just horrible.

MARGERY. I have a book, too.

ASMODEUS. Oh yes?

(**MARGERY** *opens her dress. She has* **JULIANA***'s book tucked in her garments. She takes it out and holds it tightly.*)

Ooooooooooh, pretty. Why don't you read some of that to me?

(**MARGERY** *looks down at the book in hope that it will somehow reveal its secrets to her.*)

Oh. Oh, I see. Well, why don't I read to you, then. Ahem. "In the year 1401, the witch and Lollard Margery Kempe" – oh that's you! – "was denied strangulation and burned at the stake for falsely wearing white when she was clearly not a virgin, proclaiming herself a saint, and reading from an English Bible."

ASMODEUS. *(cont.)* That last charge was unfair, I think.

"She was driven to the center of town in a cart with her hands and feet tied and then strapped to a stake atop a pile of green wood."

Green wood takes longer to burn, did you know that?

"As she was burned the crowd of her former friends hurled stones at her while screaming that she was a filthy slut who deserved to die. Her best friend, Anne was the most gleeful of the stone-throwers and in her enthusiasm managed to hit Mrs. Kempe in the eye."

MARGERY. ...

ASMODEUS. I can save you. You just have to ask me nicely.

MARGERY. ...How?

ASMODEUS. *(imitating her voice)* Please help me.

MARGERY. No, I mean –

ASMODEUS. I'm going to open my mouth very wide. And you just look inside there.

(sudden darkness)

Scene Ten

(FATHER THOMAS's cell. JOHN is holding a bottle of beer. He is a little tipsy.)

JOHN. I brought you our newest beer.

FATHER THOMAS. Thank you.

JOHN. Let's share the bottle.

(beat)

FATHER THOMAS. All right.

(FATHER THOMAS opens the bottle and passes it to JOHN. JOHN takes a drink.)

JOHN. How's your life at St. James?

FATHER THOMAS. It's well.

JOHN. You have a Christ-like love for all those smelly beggars?

FATHER THOMAS. Actually, yes.

JOHN. In my opinion, the priests up there are a gang of pirates who steal from the poor.

FATHER THOMAS. Ah.

JOHN. I know I'm just a brewer, but in my view the church is overstepping when it comes to indulgences – I can say that to you right? There are rumors that you're bit of a...*free thinker.*

FATHER THOMAS. I support the church and the true Pope.

JOHN. Do you? That's not what they say at the Gildhall.

FATHER THOMAS. I don't pay much attention to idle tongues.

JOHN. Oh yes those of us who work for a living have idle tongues while you priests slave in service to God. Cheers.

FATHER THOMAS. I thought the men at the Gildhall spent all their time getting drunk while the poor slaved in service to *them.* Did you brew that beer with your own hands, John?

JOHN. I work taking care of my son because my wife is too busy loving God to love her family.

FATHER THOMAS. Did you want to discus something specific?

JOHN. Tell my wife she has to stop wearing white.

FATHER THOMAS. You know that Margery does as she pleases.

JOHN. The whole town is laughing at her.

FATHER THOMAS. I'll speak with her but –

JOHN. She's not married to Jesus Christ, she's married to me!

FATHER THOMAS. You need to be patient with her, John.

JOHN. Why? Why the Hell should I be patient? Jesus Christ in *purple robes?*

FATHER THOMAS. I believe her.

JOHN. Why?

FATHER THOMAS. I've seen her tears.

JOHN. Obviously you don't have much experience with women.

FATHER THOMAS. John //

JOHN. She's slippery! She's a little snake! When I first met Margery, I thought, this girl is the most gorgeous thing God ever put on this earth, but I never thought she was *honest!*

FATHER THOMAS. She is honest.

JOHN. No! She's a woman and she's beautiful and that's not the same thing. For God's sakes, look deep into your heart Father.

FATHER THOMAS. I look deep into my heart every day, John.

JOHN. And what do see when you look in there? Some fucking woman! // The problem with women is they don't have to be honest because they're beautiful! They are aren't they? Aren't they? Come on, Father, confess that you think women are beautiful!

FATHER THOMAS. Please stop blaspheming.

JOHN. They're just so – Aaaaaaaaaaaaaaaah. They're incredible! With their tits and their //

FATHER THOMAS. John //

JOHN. tits! Oh God and their skin and their soft little –

FATHER THOMAS. Please.

JOHN. What? Does it excite you to much? Is it painful to keep those vows when you hear of other men's exploits?

FATHER THOMAS. Actually, my mother is in the next room.

JOHN. Oh. *(beat)* Sorry.

FATHER THOMAS. And I don't like to hear of Margery talked about in that way. She's much more to me –

JOHN. *(whispering)* Much more to *you?* What do you think she is to me? And you've stolen her from me and turned her into the most boring woman on earth.

FATHER THOMAS. Your wife is not boring.

JOHN. Oh no. She isn't? Weeping all day, refusing to eat with me, refusing to fuck me. Jumping out of bed in the middle of night to explain how merry life in Heaven is!

FATHER THOMAS. KEEP YOUR VOICE DOWN.

(beat)

JOHN. Sorry. *(resentfully)* Do you like the beer?

FATHER THOMAS. It's quite good actually.

JOHN. *(softening)* There's a bit of a burn but – thank you. This is the first good batch we've had all year. We might have to close the business – we're nearly bankrupt.

FATHER THOMAS. I'm sorry to hear that.

JOHN. Don't be polite – I know the whole town is gossiping about how demons have gotten into our horses, how God is punishing us. Whores // on the street scream, "Witch!" when she walks outside...

FATHER THOMAS. You need to be more careful with your –

JOHN. ...and we've had five men quit because she makes the workers pray and preaches to them in the evenings.

FATHER THOMAS. You have to tell her to stop preaching, it's against the law.

JOHN. She knows it's against the law and she doesn't care! And now her bitch friend //

FATHER THOMAS. John.

JOHN. Anne is telling all her other bitch friends that she's a Lollard. //

FATHER THOMAS. What?

JOHN. (Sorry. I know. I do penance for it every week.)

(beat)

FATHER THOMAS. She's not a Lollard.

JOHN. No, she's my wife!

FATHER THOMAS. Who's saying that she's a –

JOHN. Everybody! She's got no friends left! She runs around babbling about the music of Heaven.

FATHER THOMAS. Has anyone accused her, though? I mean officially.

JOHN. What?

FATHER THOMAS. They just burned a man for being a Lollard.

JOHN. Where? In France?

FATHER THOMAS. No! Nearby – in Smithfield. The Bishops are rounding up Lollards –

JOHN. My father-in-law was the mayor, no one's going to burn his daughter.

FATHER THOMAS. William Sautre was a chaplain. They don't care who her father was.

JOHN. Oh, calm down, Father.

FATHER THOMAS. Have you ever smelled burning human flesh?

JOHN. No, but I hear it smells like pork.

FATHER THOMAS. John.

JOHN. It's 1401. They don't burn women anymore!

FATHER THOMAS. The law makes no exception for women.

(beat)

JOHN. Then stop teaching her things.

FATHER THOMAS. What?

JOHN. Did you tell her she could wear white?

FATHER THOMAS. Not exactly.

JOHN. And those sermons she's preaching, does she get them from you?

FATHER THOMAS. I don't know. I read to her.

(beat)

JOHN. Have you got children?

FATHER THOMAS. What? No. Of course not.

JOHN. And you're going to Heaven, right?

FATHER THOMAS. I hope so.

JOHN. So it's not so terrible if they burn you.

(beat)

FATHER THOMAS. I'll talk to her about the way she dresses.

JOHN. Good. You can come by the house to do that. She doesn't come here.

FATHER THOMAS. ...I understand.

JOHN. Thank you. *(beat)* Can I ask you another question?

FATHER THOMAS. Yes.

JOHN. Is it true that priests have extra large...merchandise?

FATHER THOMAS. Are you drunk?

JOHN. There was some priest I heard about recently from Worms! He was screwing a married woman, driving // her insane. It's not only the size of your wares, it's that they have a special shape.

FATHER THOMAS. Alright.

Goodnight and thank you for the beer.

JOHN. I'm not that drunk!

FATHER THOMAS. I'll speak to Margery about the way she dresses.

JOHN. *(with real gratitude)* Thank you. Thank you Father. I love her.

FATHER THOMAS. I know you do.

JOHN. I love her, Father. You care about her eternal soul, but I love her here on earth.

FATHER THOMAS. I understand.

JOHN. You talk with her.

FATHER THOMAS. I will.

JOHN. Thank you. Thank you.

　　(**JOHN** *hugs* **FATHER THOMAS** *tightly then lets him go.*)

FATHER THOMAS. I do know that women are beautiful, John.

　　(**JOHN** *grabs* **FATHER THOMAS**.)

JOHN. Stay the Hell away from my wife or we'll chase you out of Lynn with torches. I can do it, Father. They respect me. I'm a respected man.

Scene Eleven

(The kitchen. **MARGERY** *prays frantically.)*

MARGERY. Please you will you visit me just one more time?
I know that you are always with me but I am forgetting your face.
And the Devil has come for me again.
Please tell me what I am to do.

*(***JOHN*** *enters, still a little tipsy.)*

JOHN. Hello, little witch.

MARGERY. Who is that? What are you?

JOHN. A demon.

MARGERY. JOHN! Don't joke about that. The Devil has come for me again.

JOHN. What?

MARGERY. He read to me from his book. He had little horns and a tail —

JOHN. No, no you dreamed it. The Devil never comes in the shape of the Devil.

MARGERY. He was wearing his costume for the mystery pageant!

JOHN. Oh, Christ.

MARGERY. He opened his mouth really wide.

JOHN. That's it. Take off that stupid dress. We're going to Father Walter.

MARGERY. Why?

JOHN. You're going to ask for his help.

MARGERY. But / / John .

JOHN. Be quiet for once and listen to me: You will say him that you're sick and your vision was just a dream.

*(***NURSE*** *enters.)*

NURSE. Here's your steak, miss.

*(***JOHN*** *pushes the steak toward* **MARGERY***.)*

MARGERY. I don't want it.

JOHN. Leave it.

MARGERY. I'm fasting.

JOHN. Eat.

(**NURSE** *exits.*)

MARGERY. It wasn't a dream. God *spoke* to me.

JOHN. Do you want them to burn you?

MARGERY. What?

JOHN. The bishops are rounding up heretics.

MARGERY. I'm not a –

JOHN. Do you know a church official who will vouch for you?

MARGERY. Father Thomas says —

JOHN. He's not a real priest! He helps the poor!

MARGERY. My Father was the Mayor of Lynn four –

JOHN. No one cares who your father was! They just killed a man in Smithfield —

MARGERY. I'm not a Lollard!

(*beat*)

JOHN. Please, little frog. Come here. Just tell Father Walter that your vision wasn't real and then you can stay home here with me and the baby.

MARGERY. I can't lie. It's a sin to lie.

JOHN. Why don't you think for a moment about how it long takes to be burned alive.

MARGERY. …

JOHN. Now you're frightened.

MARGERY. No, I'm not. I'm just hungry.

JOHN. Why don't you eat then?

(**JOHN** *tries to feed her a piece of steak.*)

JOHN. Why don't you eat if you're hungry?

MARGERY. It's not what God wants from me.

JOHN. But what about you?

MARGERY. Let me be!

JOHN. Have you no mind of your own, little frog? What do you want?

MARGERY. *(spitting out the food)* My mind is not separate from God's!

JOHN. EAT! EAT YOU STUPID BITCH! EAT!

(NURSE enters.)

NURSE. Excuse me, miss.

JOHN. WHAT IS IT?

NURSE. Mrs. Kempe wanted me to tell her when it was time to go to church.

JOHN. She's not going to church.

MARGERY. Yes, I am.

JOHN. No, she's staying home.

MARGERY. Thank you, Eliza.

(JOHN grabs at her.)

JOHN. Please Margery. Please just love me. Just love me again.

(MARGERY enjoys this for a brief moment for a moment. Then pulls away.)

MARGERY. *(to God)* Smite off his head if he touches me!

JOHN. Do you mean that?

MARGERY. …

JOHN. I'm your husband.

MARGERY. I belong to God.

(long silence)

JOHN. He can have you, then.

Scene Twelve

(NURSE's room. NURSE is singing to the baby.)

NURSE.

BIRD ON BRIAR, BIRD, BIRD ON BRIAR!
WE'RE BORN OF LOVE, AND LOVE WE CRAVE.
HAVE PITY, BIRD, AND QUENCH MY FIRE,
OR MAKE, DEAR LOVE, MAKE ME MY GRAVE.

Scene Thirteen

(FATHER THOMAS's cell. MARGERY kneels before FATHER
THOMAS.)

FATHER THOMAS. It's after midnight! You can't stay here.

MARGERY. My husband says I have to stop wearing white.

FATHER THOMAS. Go back home, Margery. We'll speak to-
morrow.

MARGERY. He wants me to say my vision was just a dream!

FATHER THOMAS. You should do as he says.

MARGERY. What?

FATHER THOMAS. He loves you. He will keep you safe.

MARGERY. But God sent you to be my teacher!

FATHER THOMAS. I don't know if that's true.

(beat)

I have looked deeply into my heart and now I see that
I have no genuine understanding what it is that God is
asking of me. Perhaps it is because he is asking nothing.

MARGERY. "This world is pregnant with God!"

FATHER THOMAS. Are you laughing at me?

MARGERY. No. No. Your revelation – "This world // is..."

FATHER THOMAS. Margery, go home to your family.

MARGERY. I am God's servant!

FATHER THOMAS. You're also a wife. And a mother.

MARGERY. You don't think I should wear white?

FATHER THOMAS. No, I don't.

MARGERY. Oh…

(beat)

I know that God sent you to be my teacher. I'll do whatever you ask.

FATHER THOMAS. Thank you.

MARGERY. I will lie about my vision, if that's what you are
asking me to do.

FATHER THOMAS. Margery –

MARGERY. But please tell me, if I lie and they burn me, what will happen to my soul?

FATHER THOMAS. …

MARGERY. Forgive me Father, for I have sinned —

FATHER THOMAS. What are you doing?

MARGERY. When I was ten years old —

FATHER THOMAS. You need to go back home. What if some-one finds you here?

MARGERY. You said you would hear my confession.

FATHER THOMAS. No, Margery, I'm sorry, I can't —

MARGERY. If they burn me, what will happen to my soul?

FATHER THOMAS. They won't burn you! Please, just listen to your husband and all will be well.

MARGERY. Forgive me Father, when I was ten years old —

FATHER THOMAS. I can't hear your confession!

MARGERY. Why not?

FATHER THOMAS. I don't know if I am entirely… *(beat)* Forgive me.

(beat)

MARGERY. Of course I forgive you. Since my mind is also twisted by the Devil. Every day he torments me with the same game. Do you want to know what it is? Well in this game I'm naked!

FATHER THOMAS. Margery. Please go —

MARGERY. I'm naked and I'm standing in front of a line of ten priests // and they're all naked too, and the devil he's standing behind me and he says, "Margery! Choose one!"

FATHER THOMAS. You should go.

MARGERY. *(mocking him)* And do you know what the worst part is, Father? It doesn't matter which priest I like the best – because eventually the devil is going to make me fuck every single priest!

Can you believe that? Isn't that horrible? Please help me Father – what should I do? What.

*(**MARGERY** looks at him with scorn.)*

FATHER THOMAS. It is his will and plan that we hang on to him...

(MARGERY exits. FATHER THOMAS kneels to pray. He cannot. He finds the bag of figs MARGERY left for his mother and begins to violently stuff them in his mouth.)

NURSE. Excuse me, Father. Could you please tell me, is there such a thing as witchcraft?

FATHER THOMAS. *(quickly covering his mouth)* Hm? What?!

NURSE. Are you well, sir?

FATHER THOMAS. Yes. What are you doing here?

NURSE. Following Mrs. Kempe. How does a woman know if she is witch? Is there a test she can do?

FATHER THOMAS. Mrs. Kempe is not a witch.

NURSE. *(removing a pouch from her pocket)* I know that. I'm speaking about my sister. She cast a spell with these chicken bones but something went wrong with the spell and she has caused great harm. Is there something she can do to reverse it?

FATHER THOMAS. That is not my area of study.

NURSE. But can you help her purify herself? They are arresting witches now.

FATHER THOMAS. Yes. It's a thrilling time.

NURSE. Are you teasing me, sir?

FATHER THOMAS. Yes, I am. When I said "thrilling" I meant "bloodthirsty" – but don't tell anyone I said that and I won't tell anyone your sister is a witch.

NURSE. My sister's not a –

FATHER THOMAS. I know.

NURSE. Here please take these bones.

(FATHER THOMAS reluctantly takes them.)

NURSE. Can you take the power out of them.

FATHER THOMAS. They have no power. They're just bones.

NURSE. Couldn't you give my sister some penance to do?

FATHER THOMAS. No.

NURSE. Or a bit of teaching?

FATHER THOMAS. ...

NURSE. Sir?

FATHER THOMAS. Tell your sister that once, a certain priest was on a journey and he got lost in a dark wood. Then, the middle of a clearing he saw a pear tree, covered in luminous blossoms. He could not take his eyes from this tree all night long and finally in the morning, he ran up shook the branches so hard that all the blossoms fell to the ground and then he hungrily ate every last one. After he had eaten his fill do you know what he did?

NURSE. No.

FATHER THOMAS. He squatted on the ground, and shit out all of all the flowers he had so greedily devoured.

NURSE. Father?

FATHER THOMAS. Please go. I'm so tired.

NURSE. Figs are not good for men. They aggravate the spleen. You might try cucumber or fennel as a remedy.

(**NURSE** *exits.*)

FATHER THOMAS. *(tasting the figs in his mouth)* Pah pah pah. Oh dear God.

(**FATHER THOMAS** *begins to retch violently.*)

Scene Fourteen

(Early morning. **JACOB** *stands alone inside St. Margaret's church. He looks around nervously. He hears a sound. It's nothing.* **MARGERY** *enters.)*

JACOB. I was waiting for you for over an hour.

MARGERY. Will you hear my confession?

JACOB. What?

MARGERY. There is a sin I have been carrying in my heart.

JACOB. You can't confess to me. It's against the law.

MARGERY. No, if a priest cannot be found, sins can be confessed to a friend.

JACOB. Really?

MARGERY. You are my friend, aren't you?

(beat)

JACOB. Yes. How do I do it?

MARGERY. Um. Just bow your head.

JACOB. Don't I need a Bible?

MARGERY. I don't think so.

JACOB. I'm pretty sure I need a –

MARGERY. Here use this.

(She hands him **JULIANA***'s book. He looks at it.)*

JACOB. Now what do I do?

MARGERY. You just listen.

JACOB. ...I'm listening.

MARGERY. Forgive me...friend, for I have sinned. When I was –

JACOB. Wait.

MARGERY. Yes?

JACOB. Is it really horrible?

MARGERY. ...

JACOB. I'm sorry. Of course it's not horrible. I have never known a woman as perfect as you.

MARGERY. ...

JACOB. I'm listening.

MARGERY. I think I'd like to wait.

JACOB. No, please. Let me help you.

(beat)

MARGERY. Will you take me out of Lynn?

JACOB. What?

MARGERY. Father Walter wants to burn me.

JACOB. I would do anything for you. I would cut my heart out of my chest and put it on a plate for // you to...

MARGERY. I know.

JACOB. I'll take you to a little house on the outskirts of town.

MARGERY. On the outskirts of –

JACOB. Yes, I'll sneak out at night to find us food. And during the days we will worship Him together. I will read to you only of God, of how much He loves you and how miraculous you are.

*(**MARGERY** kisses him.)*

You're tempting me.

*(**MARGERY** kisses him again.)*

Why are you tempting me?

*(They kiss. **JACOB** lurches suddenly out of her arms.)*

MARGERY. Forgive me.

JACOB. My mother told me the Devil never comes as the devil. He often comes as a woman. Especially an older woman!

MARGERY. You're bleeding.

JACOB. Ach! I'm bleeding! I'm bleeding!

MARGERY. Let me help you.

JACOB. You have infected me with your mouth! I'M BLEEDING!

MARGERY. Forgive me.

JACOB. My friends all told me that you were a fraud and now I know they were right.

MARGERY. No, you know me.

JACOB. I wonder if they'll use green wood to burn you?

(*JACOB exits.* MARGERY *kneels to pray.*)

MARGERY. All that I am and all that I possess, You have given me. I surrender it all to you. I'm sorry that I am so weak, but I miss you. I miss your sweet face. I don't know if I can go on living in your absence? Give me only your love and I will desire nothing more.

(*A low rumbling sound.* MARGERY *sits up and looks toward Heaven.*)

Hello? Oh, yes. Yes. Tell me what I am to do. Give me a sign.

(*A deafening clamor as the church ceiling collapses on top of* MARGERY. *Darkness.*)

Scene Sixteen

(The cell of JULIANA *of Norwich.* JULIANA*'s voice is heard in the darkness until a flood of light reveals her sitting alone. She reads from the book of a Benedictine nun.)*

JULIANA. "When the human form emerged from the woman's womb, it changed color depending on the movement that the soul – which was a ball of fire – made within it. And I saw how many storms assailed this human and weighed it down to the ground. And I saw that as this human body tried to raise itself up, it said with a groan:"

*(*MARGERY *enters* JULIANA*'s cell. She is still wearing her white dress, but it has torn at the knees. She wears a bandage around her head.)*

"A stranger, where am I? In the shadow of death. Which path am I traveling? The path of error. What consolations do I have? The consolation of the pilgrim in exile."

*(*MARGERY *covers her mouth and begins to cough.* JULIANA *closes the book.)*

No matter how often I wash, it always reeks of flesh. Here's lavender. Put it under your nose.

*(*MARGERY *takes the lavender and dabs it under her nose.)*

You'll get accustomed.

MARGERY. *(timidly)* …one of your windows looks into the church.

JULIANA. Yes but it's a horrible view. Look, I can barely see the pulpit. Savages. Giving me such a miserable view of God. I'm teasing. I'm only teasing. Sit down there. That's where Mathilda used to sit. My cat. Sometimes I wake in the middle of the night and I see her there. That sounds witchy doesn't it? Don't tell anyone I said that.

MARGERY. I won't.

JULIANA. What is your name again? Just keep dabbing under your nose.

MARGERY. *(dabbing under her nose)* Margery...Kempe.

JULIANA. Now, Margery, when you begin to tell your vision, I'm going to close my eyes, do you mind? I have such painful headaches. So it was a vision of what – Christ I suppose?

MARGERY. *(shy)* Well, yes. But it was nothing like your visions.

JULIANA. Oh I don't have visions anymore (well sometimes I have visions of Mathilda). No, no I had all my visions thirty years ago and they all happened in one night – (can you imagine?) – sixteen of them in three hours. And now I've spent the rest of my life locked in here trying to figure out what they meant.

MARGERY. Oh.

JULIANA. Could I get you something to eat before you tell me your vision?

MARGERY. No, thank you. I'm fasting.

JULIANA. Let's share this pomegranate. Someone brought it to the window. They bring the strangest things from their pilgrimages. (Probably came straight from some Muslim's orchard don't you think?) Look out there for a moment. Do you see a red-haired girl?

MARGERY. No.

JULIANA. Are you sure?

MARGERY. I don't. I don't see anyone.

JULIANA. She's completely cracked! She sleeps outside my window for days and she won't take food or water. Rebelling against her family I suppose. (Wealthy girls!) Here take this half. It's bloody, isn't it? Take it! Fasting is all well but let's not indulge it every moment. Eating with me that's holy, too. Unless I'm a witch of course. Then you're damned. Don't look at me like that. I'm not a witch. Why do you fast?

MARGERY. ...to relieve the suffering of sinners who are in purgatory.

JULIANA. Yes of course, but do you have any one in particular in mind?

MARGERY. ...My father.

JULIANA. Well that's good of you. But purgatory's not Hell you know. It's just waiting. It's just remaining patient – which is after all what is required of us here, too. What's his name?

MARGERY. John Brunham.

JULIANA. It's so tiresome, isn't it? If only we were accountable for strictly our own sins wouldn't that be so much easier?

MARGERY. Yes.

JULIANA. Well, I don't believe that. I don't believe it would be easier.

MARGERY. Oh.

JULIANA. Eat.

MARGERY. Thank you.

   (**MARGERY** *bites awkwardly into the pomegranate.*)

JULIANA. No dear. Just one seed at a time. There you go. "Thank you, John Brunham, for waiting one more day that we might enjoy this pomegranate!"

MARGERY. Oh yes, shall we pray?

JULIANA. You may pray if you like. I don't consider it a separate activity.

   (**MARGERY** *reluctantly begins to lie on her back.*)

MARGERY. Excuse me.

JULIANA. Do you perceive Him better on your back then?

MARGERY. Yes.

JULIANA. I perceived Him only in sickness. When I was young and an idiot, I prayed for Him to give me a mortal sickness. You've never prayed for that have you?

MARGERY. No.

JULIANA. Good girl. I was stupid. I wanted to understand what it was to die, and by understanding that come to know Him. I was no older than that little red-haired witch – check out there one more time please. She's there isn't she?

MARGERY. *(getting up to look)* ...No.

JULIANA. Ten years passed and I completely forgot that I had ever asked for such a foolish thing. And then when I was thirty, God sent me the terrible sickness I had requested! (He has a wonderful memory, God.) I lay dying for three days and three nights, and in the darkness lurked hundreds of demons...but then suddenly I was totally well and I had sixteen visions in the course of an hour! And that was it! It was all over!

MARGERY. Have you prayed for more?

JULIANA. No. Noooooooooo. I don't want *more*! My mind is already too burdened thinking about those sixteen. The sixteenth itself was especially confusing. What's your name again?

MARGERY. Margery.

JULIANA. What was your vision, Margery?

MARGERY. Um.

JULIANA. I'll close my eyes and you tell me, dear. *(She closes her eyes.)* I'm not sleeping! I want to hear!

MARGERY. Well. The night my baby was born –

JULIANA. Oh, you have a baby!

MARGERY. What? Oh? Yes. I do.

JULIANA. Boy or girl?

MARGERY. Um, boy.

JULIANA. Oh, I love babies. Sometimes I would hold Matilda in my arms like she was a baby – I couldn't hold her for long, because cats like to be free, but – I taught her the word nose, too. I would hold her in my arms like a baby and then I would point at my nose and say "nose, nose" and one day I said "nose" and she lifted her paw and put it right on my nose! Can you imagine? Anyway, go on.

(JULIANA *closes her eyes.*)

MARGERY. The night my baby was born I sent for a priest –

JULIANA. To bless your baby!

MARGERY. Well, yes, and also because there was something serious I needed to confess.

JULIANA. *(opening her eyes)* Oh.

MARGERY. But as soon as I began to speak, the priest, Father Walter, put his hand over my mouth and told me there was no need for me to confess because I was going to Hell anyway. And he ran out the door.

JULIANA. Hm.

MARGERY. Suddenly, the devil was on my bed with his claw around my throat…And then, he opened his mouth.

JULIANA. Ah.

MARGERY. I've seen what Hell is like and I can't go there.

JULIANA. …

MARGERY. *(uncertain)* But then one night I heard a knocking on the door…and God's son walked into my room and sat on my bed. He was wearing purple robes.

JULIANA. Oooh.

MARGERY. And He took me in His…in the arms…of His soul and He said: "Why have you left me, child, when I never for a moment went away from you?"

(Silence. MARGERY *looks to* JULIANA *nervously.)*

JULIANA. It's a respectable vision.

MARGERY. Truly? It's so simple.

JULIANA. Yes. Well. Congratulations. The Bishop will give you my certificate. Just make certain he puts his signature below mine. It never hurts to have a second signature.

MARGERY. I should tell you that the Devil has started visiting me again.

JULIANA. It's his duty to be persistent.

MARGERY. And I am almost constantly troubled with horrible temptations of flesh.

JULIANA. Oh well. Temptations of flesh. Why do you think I lock myself in here?

MARGERY. ...

JULIANA. *This* window looks into the church. *This* window here is where I give my confessions. And do you see this third window? This is the window that looks out onto the world. This third window tortures me. It's a constant daily effort to love this window as little as I can. Sometimes a creature will be mad enough to put its soft little hand out toward the window and you can't imagine how difficult it is some days not to grab it and kiss it. What happened to your head?

MARGERY. *(ashamed)* The church ceiling fell on me while I was praying.

JULIANA. Oh! I'm sorry. I'm sorry. You're so serious.

MARGERY. And then I walked here all the way from Lynn.

JULIANA. By yourself?

MARGERY. Yes!

JULIANA. Good girl! Why?

MARGERY. They want to burn me.

JULIANA. Oh they want to burn everybody now. Right across the river over there, they've started burning. Sometimes I can smell the smoke at night. It seeps in through the cracks and I – Nevermind. I'm letting that thought go for now. You see, I say hello to the thought and then I let it go. Goodbye. Don't worry. They won't burn you now. Every one respects me. I have no idea why but – actually I'm being modest. My book – you know my book?

MARGERY. Oh yes. I have it right here.

JULIANA. Oh lovely. Here I'll sign it and then you should probably be going.

(She writes for quite some time. She returns the book to **MARGERY***.)*

JULIANA. It was wonderful to meet –

MARGERY. Would you hear my confession?

JULIANA. Ooooh. Forgive me, but I can't. It could inflame my passions. Too much excitement, you understand. Sometimes I think that Confession was invented just to give the poor priests a little taste of life. Oh, don't cry. No no. Come here. Come here. Sit here beside me. Do you know how to meditate?

MARGERY. Yes.

JULIANA. Close your eyes. I'll pet your hair like this, like your mother used to. Did your mother used to do this?

MARGERY. Yes.

(JULIANA *begins to pet* MARGERY's *hair again.*)

JULIANA. Are you meditating?

MARGERY. ...Yes.

JULIANA. Good. Now, think of your mother's face.

(*She waits for* MARGERY *to do this.*)

Remember the face you knew as a little baby. Do you her see her eyes? Do you see how tenderly they look at you?

(*She waits for* MARGERY *to remember.*)

Do you see how more than anything in the world she wishes no harm ever to come to you? Do you see how her eyes hold onto you in your entirety? Do you see that you are enclosed within her gaze and do you see that her gaze is actually a world, *an entire world of its own*, the very world in which you are enfolded and embraced?

(MARGERY *lays her head in* JULIANA's *lap.*)

JULIANA. Do you see her face?

MARGERY. ...Yes.

JULIANA. Now I'll tell you a secret: I don't believe in Hell. I have tried for many years, but with great agony I have finally set aside this belief. And what is so terrible, really, about this Hell? What is it that terrifies you really? the fires? The hot pokers? The animals chewing holes in our flesh? (*laughing*) No, no. Sin itself is what is terrifying. If you had to choose between all the pains of this place they call "Hell" and Sin, I promise you that you would choose all that pain rather than Sin. Do you know what Sin is?

MARGERY. The evil that we do?

JULIANA. No, no that's such a little thing, the evil that we do – it's so tiny, it's as tiny as we are. True Sin is the terrible distance between ourselves and God. There is no harder Hell than this. Do you still see your mother's face?

MARGERY. Yes.

JULIANA. Try to remember that face when you are thinking of God.

(knocking on the window)

Oh it's her again. No, don't move. Just rest for a moment. We'll let her knock.

(The knocking continues.)

We'll let her knock and knock and then we'll open the door and we'll let her in.

Scene Sixteen

(Lynn. Outside the Kempe's home)

(She looks all around.)

MARGERY. Look at all that smoke. The whole town is burning. I know that I asked you to burn up all of my
enemies but please show them forgiveness —

(She sees the cradle.)

I can almost see you now. I can almost see your sweet
face.

Please have mercy on my little child.

My child.

(She runs to it. She lowers it. There is no baby inside.)

(JOHN appears holding the baby.)

JOHN. *(to the baby)* Look. Your mother's home.

(The baby begins crying.)

Oh no. No. Shhhhhhhhh. Shhhhhhhhhhhhh. Don't
cry. He's just frightened by the fire.

MARGERY. ...May I hold him?

JOHN. *(surprised)* Yes. Yes. Like this.

(He hands her the baby. She takes him awkwardly.)

MARGERY. He smells so sweet. I didn't know they smelled
like this. Am I hurting him?

JOHN. Just rest him against your body. I was so worried
about you.

MARGERY. I walked all the way to Norwich. I'm not a heretic. I got my certificate.

JOHN. I heard.

MARGERY. Now I can weep as loudly as I want. He's heavy.

JOHN. He's a little man already. We'll have to camp out
here until morning.

MARGERY. Did Father Thomas – ?

JOHN. He took his mother to Leicester.

MARGERY. Thank God. *(to the baby)* Hello. Hello. He doesn't like me.

JOHN. He doesn't know you, yet.

MARGERY. Oh. I felt something on my cheek. Is that rain?

JOHN. I didn't feel anything. It's cold out here. Let me hold you.

(He puts his arms around her. She leans back against him, rocking the baby.)

I felt something on my cheek, too.

MARGERY. Look. It's snowing. *(to the baby)* It's snowing.

JOHN. *(to the baby)* It's snowing!

MARGERY. *(to the baby)* Hello, you fat little Creature. I am your mother. He's laughing at me.

JOHN. I can't believe you walked to Norwich all by yourself.

MARGERY. Well, I hired a beggar to carry my bag but he didn't like my praying and quit after the first hour. Why did Father Thomas go Leicester?

JOHN. They found an English Bible in his house.

MARGERY. Will they burn him?

JOHN. Unless he can find a way out of England. *(beat)* Margery?

MARGERY. ...I'm cold. Let's walk a little toward the fire.

JOHN. All right.

(JOHN puts his arm around her and they start to walk. MARGERY stops for a moment and looks down at the baby.)

MARGERY. I can't endure it. When I think of his suffering... How will I endure it?

JOHN. Let me hold onto you.

(They begin walk toward the fire. Darkness grows behind them as the light in front of them grows brighter and sparks begin to fly. A shape emerges from a blanket. It is ASMODEUS dressed in rags, his face charred.)

ASMODEUS. Margery is that you? I hear your voice! I hear it! MARGERY. Oh look there is that her? Yes, yes, yes, yes, yes, yes I can tell by her funny little walk. Oooooooooooh I could look at her forever. She's a miracle.

End of Play

OTHER TITLES AVAILABLE FROM SAMUEL FRENCH

SMUDGE

Rachel Axler

2m, 1f / Dark Comedy / Interior

A dark comedy about the changing face of the American family and the limits of love and cheesecake, as a hopeful young couple gives birth to a smudge, written by two-time Emmy Award winner Rachel Axler.

"For signs of intelligent life in the theatrical universe, I hereby refer you to *Smudge*, Rachel Axler's pitch-black comedy."
– Marilyn Stasio, *Variety*

"Creepy and funny. Precise and imaginative. Parenthood never looked weirder or more terrifying than it does in *Smudge*"
– Rachel Saltz, *The New York Times*

"The mysterious newborn in Rachel Axler's smart, piquant *Smudge* is not lovable-looking... In some sense, Axler's dark comedy is a horror story: a parent's nightmare rendered with sometimes lyrical surrealism. A meditation on ambiguity and ambivalence, *Smudge* also illustrates ambition: a parent's, thwarted, and a playwright's, achieved."
– Adam Feldman, *Time Out New York*

"*Smudge* is filled with laughs, due to Rachel Axler's tart way with quips, director Pam MacKinnon's brisk, unsentimental touch, and the ability of both Greg Keller and Cassie Beck to make their characters real and complex."
– Jennifer Farrar, *Associated Press*

"An ambitious play, one that ponders such big questions as how to communicate and what it means to be alive. A play that sticks with you, both for its laughs and for its message."
– Julia Furay, *CurtainUp*